Francis Frith's
Stourbridge
Living Memories

Photographic Memories

Francis Frith's
Stourbridge
Living Memories

Dorothy Nicolle

First published in the United Kingdom in 2002 by
Frith Book Company Ltd

Paperback Edition 2002
ISBN 1-85937-530-8

British Library Cataloguing in Publication Data

Francis Frith's Stourbridge Living Memories
Dorothy Nicolle

Frith Book Company Ltd
Frith's Barn, Teffont,
Salisbury, Wiltshire SP3 5QP
Tel: +44 (0) 1722 716 376
Email: info@francisfrith.co.uk
www.francisfrith.co.uk

Printed and bound in Great Britain

Front Cover: **Stourbridge, High Street 1931** 84687

Contents

Francis Frith: *Victorian Pioneer*

FRANCIS FRITH, Victorian founder of the world-famous photographic archive, was a complex and multi-talented man. A devout Quaker and a highly successful Victorian businessman, he was both philosophic by nature and pioneering in outlook.

By 1855 Francis Frith had already established a wholesale grocery business in Liverpool, and sold it for the astonishing sum of £200,000, which is the equivalent today of over £15,000,000. Now a multi-millionaire, he was able to indulge his passion for travel. As a child he had pored over travel books written by early explorers, and his fancy and imagination had been stirred by family holidays to the sublime mountain regions of Wales and Scotland. 'What a land of spirit-stirring and enriching scenes and places!' he had written. He was to return to these scenes of grandeur in later years to 'recapture the thousands of vivid and tender memories', but with a different purpose. Now in his thirties, and captivated by the new science of photography, Frith set out on a series of pioneering journeys to the Nile regions that occupied him from 1856 until 1860.

Intrigue and Adventure

He took with him on his travels a specially-designed wicker carriage that acted as both dark-room and sleeping chamber. These far-flung journeys were packed with intrigue and adventure. In his life story, written when he was sixty-three, Frith tells of being held captive by bandits, and of fighting 'an awful midnight battle to the very point of surrender with a deadly pack of hungry, wild dogs'. Sporting flowing Arab costume, Frith arrived at Akaba by camel seventy years before Lawrence, where he encountered 'desert princes and rival sheikhs, blazing with jewel-hilted swords'.

During these extraordinary adventures he was assiduously exploring the desert regions bordering the Nile and patiently recording the antiquities and peoples with his camera. He was the first photographer to venture beyond the sixth cataract. Africa was still the mysterious 'Dark Continent', and Stanley and Livingstone's historic meeting was a decade into the future. The conditions for picture taking confound belief. He laboured for hours in his wicker dark-room in the sweltering heat of the desert, while the volatile chemicals fizzed dangerously in their trays. Often he was forced to work in remote tombs and caves where conditions were cooler. Back in London he exhibited his photographs and was 'rapturously cheered' by members of the Royal Society. His reputation as a photographer was made overnight. An eminent modern historian has likened their impact on the population of the time to that on our own generation of the first photographs taken on the surface of the moon.

Venture of a Life-Time

Characteristically, Frith quickly spotted the opportunity to create a new business as a specialist publisher of photographs. He lived in an era of immense and sometimes violent change. For the poor in the early part of Victoria's reign work was a drudge and the hours long, and people had precious little free time to enjoy themselves. Most had no transport other than a cart or gig at their disposal, and had not travelled far beyond the boundaries of their own town or village. However,

by the 1870s, the railways had threaded their way across the country, and Bank Holidays and half-day Saturdays had been made obligatory by Act of Parliament. All of a sudden the ordinary working man and his family were able to enjoy days out and see a little more of the world.

With characteristic business acumen, Francis Frith foresaw that these new tourists would enjoy having souvenirs to commemorate their days out. In 1860 he married Mary Ann Rosling and set out with the intention of photographing every city, town and village in Britain. For the next thirty years he travelled the country by train and by pony and trap, producing fine photographs of seaside resorts and beauty spots that were keenly bought by millions of Victorians. These prints were painstakingly pasted into family albums and pored over during the dark nights of winter, rekindling precious memories of summer excursions.

The Rise of Frith & Co

Frith's studio was soon supplying retail shops all over the country. To meet the demand he gathered about him a small team of photographers, and published the work of independent artist-photographers of the calibre of Roger Fenton and Francis Bedford. In order to gain some understanding of the scale of Frith's business one only has to look at the catalogue issued by Frith & Co in 1886: it runs to some 670 pages, listing not only many thousands of views of the British Isles but also many photographs of most European countries, and China, Japan, the USA and Canada — note the sample page shown above from the hand-written *Frith & Co* ledgers detailing pictures taken. By 1890 Frith had created the greatest specialist photographic publishing company in the world,

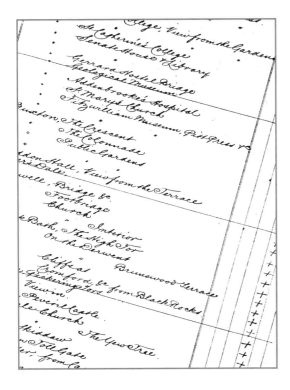

Frith's death, a new card measuring 5.5 x 3.5 inches became the standard format, but it was not until 1902 that the divided back came into being, with address and message on one face and a full-size illustration on the other. *Frith & Co* were in the vanguard of postcard development, and Frith's sons Eustace and Cyril continued their father's monumental task, expanding the number of views offered to the public and recording more and more places in Britain, as the coasts and countryside were opened up to mass travel.

Francis Frith died in 1898 at his villa in Cannes, his great project still growing. The archive he created continued in business for another seventy years. By 1970 it contained over a third of a million pictures of 7,000 cities, towns and villages. The massive photographic record Frith has left to us stands as a living monument to a special and very remarkable man.

with over 2,000 outlets – more than the combined number that Boots and W H Smith have today! The picture on the right shows the *Frith & Co* display board at Ingleton in the Yorkshire Dales. Beautifully constructed with mahogany frame and gilt inserts, it could display up to a dozen local scenes.

Postcard Bonanza

The ever-popular holiday postcard we know today took many years to develop. In 1870 the Post Office issued the first plain cards, with a pre-printed stamp on one face. In 1894 they allowed other publishers' cards to be sent through the mail with an attached adhesive halfpenny stamp. Demand grew rapidly, and in 1895 a new size of postcard was permitted called the court card, but there was little room for illustration. In 1899, a year after

Frith's Archive: *A Unique Legacy*

FRANCIS FRITH'S legacy to us today is of immense significance and value, for the magnificent archive of evocative photographs he created provides a unique record of change in 7,000 cities, towns and villages throughout Britain over a century and more. Frith and his fellow studio photographers revisited locations many times down the years to update their views, compiling for us an enthralling and colourful pageant of British life and character.

We tend to think of Frith's sepia views of Britain as nostalgic, for most of us use them to conjure up memories of places in our own lives with which we have family associations. It often makes us forget that to Francis Frith they were records of daily life as it was actually being lived in the cities, towns and villages of his day. The Victorian age was one of great and often bewildering change for ordinary people, and though the pictures evoke an impression of slower times, life was as busy and hectic as it is today.

We are fortunate that Frith was a photographer of the people, dedicated to recording the minutiae of everyday life. For it is this sheer wealth of visual data, the painstaking chronicle of changes in dress, transport, street layouts, buildings, housing, engineering and landscape that captivates us so much today. His remarkable images offer us a powerful link with the past and with the lives of our ancestors.

Today's Technology

Computers have now made it possible for Frith's many thousands of images to be accessed almost instantly. In the Frith archive today, each photograph is carefully 'digitised' then stored on a CD Rom. Frith archivists can locate a single photograph amongst thousands within seconds. Views can be catalogued and sorted under a variety of categories of place and content to the immediate benefit of researchers.

Inexpensive reference prints can be created for them at the touch of a mouse button, and a wide range of books and other printed materials assembled and published for a wider, more general readership - in the next twelve months over a hundred Frith local history titles will be published! The day-to-day workings of the archive are very different from how they were in Francis Frith's time: imagine the herculean task of sorting through eleven tons of glass negatives as Frith had to do to locate a particular sequence of pictures! Yet

See Frith at www.francisfrith.co.uk

the archive still prides itself on maintaining the same high standards of excellence laid down by Francis Frith, including the painstaking cataloguing and indexing of every view.

It is curious to reflect on how the internet now allows researchers in America and elsewhere greater instant access to the archive than Frith himself ever enjoyed. Many thousands of individual views can be called up on screen within seconds on one of the Frith internet sites, enabling people living continents away to revisit the streets of their ancestral home town, or view places in Britain where they have enjoyed holidays. Many overseas researchers welcome the chance to view special theme selections, such as transport, sports, costume and ancient monuments.

We are certain that Francis Frith would have heartily approved of these modern developments in imaging techniques, for he himself was always working at the very limits of Victorian photographic technology.

The Value of the Archive Today

Because of the benefits brought by the computer, Frith's images are increasingly studied by social historians, by researchers into genealogy and ancestory, by architects, town planners, and by teachers and schoolchildren involved in local history projects.

In addition, the archive offers every one of us an opportunity to examine the places where we and our families have lived and worked down the years. Highly successful in Frith's own era, the archive is now, a century and more on, entering a new phase of popularity.

The Past in Tune with the Future

Historians consider the Francis Frith Collection to be of prime national importance. It is the only archive of its kind remaining in private ownership and has been valued at a million pounds. However, this figure is now rapidly increasing as digital technology enables more and more people around the world to enjoy its benefits.

Francis Frith's archive is now housed in an historic timber barn in the beautiful village of Teffont in Wiltshire. Its founder would not recognize the archive office as it is today. In place of the many thousands of dusty boxes containing glass plate negatives and an all-pervading odour of photographic chemicals, there are now ranks of computer screens. He would be amazed to watch his images travelling round the world at unimaginable speeds through network and internet lines.

The archive's future is both bright and exciting. Francis Frith, with his unshakeable belief in making photographs available to the greatest number of people, would undoubtedly approve of what is being done today with his lifetime's work. His photographs, depicting our shared past, are now bringing pleasure and enlightenment to millions around the world a century and more after his death.

Stourbridge - *An Introduction*

Stourbridge is relatively unusual amongst English towns in that it was founded quite late in our history - probably not until around the 13th or possibly the 14th century. In fact, the very first mention of any settlement of that name is in a document that is dated to AD 1333.

But that is not to say that there was no-one living in the area at all. From Saxon times there was a settlement here called Swinford - 'the place where there is a ford where pigs can cross the river'. Despite its name, Swinford was actually a little distance from the river; perhaps those early settlers chose to live on higher ground. Here they were not only above the flood plain of the River Stour, but also where the grazing might have been better for the pigs they obviously owned.

Pigs must have been an important source of wealth for the local people at that time. Only a few miles to the north there is another, very similar, placename - Kingswinford. To further distinguish the two settlements, Swinford came to be known as Old Swinford, presumably because it was the earlier of the two. In fact the two words are often written as one - Oldswinford.

Old Swinford became an important settlement in its own right. However, as time passed a need grew for a convenient market place closer to where people crossed over the river; so at some point Stourbridge was established, and rapidly outgrew its parent. We know that Stourbridge was granted a charter in 1482 to hold a weekly market every Friday, but it is quite possible that there had been other such charters before this.

What was being traded in these markets? Pigs and other livestock, obviously. An early industry in the area was the production of leather, and this must have been based on livestock that was reared locally. But in medieval England one of the major commodities that was traded all over the country was wool, and this, too, was probably bought and sold in Stourbridge. Wool is unlikely to have been the main commodity traded in Stourbridge, although certainly by the 1600s woollen cloth was being produced here. Stourbridge consequently grew up to be typical of many market towns all over the country by trading in a variety of goods.

However, its proximity to the industrial heartland of Britain, the area that we now call the Black Country, was to have a particularly strong effect on Stourbridge, and it soon began to develop similar industries of its own. Early industries in the area included mining for coal and fireclay, particularly to the north and east around Brierley Hill and Lye. Lye, for example, was to become especially well known for the production of bricks: by the mid 1800s around 14 million firebricks each year were being produced in this region.

Like the nearby Black Country, Stourbridge and its neighbouring towns produced iron products too. For example, another early industry locally was the production of chains and cables. By the 1800s one ironworking company, Bradleys, had become so large that it was described as 'the largest complex of any (such) ... and perhaps the most so of any in England'. This company was to achieve special fame building steam locomotives; one of them, the Stourbridge Lion, was to be the first ever to run on rails in America. Unfortunately that particular locomotive was so heavy that it was really too much for the rails to carry. It was therefore soon abandoned. Parts were taken for other purposes, and today only its boiler and one or two other bits survive - they can be found in the Smithsonian Museum in Washington!

Coal, bricks and iron goods are heavy products to carry to customers; so once the idea of canals was first introduced, it was not long before they were being built to serve this region too. In fact the idea for a canal here had first been broached as early as the mid 1600s, when a man called Andrew Yarranton began to make the River Stour navigable around Kidderminster. He also had plans to dig canals to link the Stour with the River Trent to the north, but he was unable to follow them through for lack of funds.

Thus, the first proper canal to be built here was the Staffordshire and Worcestershire Canal, which follows a path alongside the River Stour and on northwards to Wolverhampton. It was opened in 1772, having cost £103,000 to build, a vast sum in those days. But this canal did not come to the town, and so within a few years an additional length of canal was dug so that the town of Stourbridge could be linked into the system. This canal, the

Stourbridge Canal, joined the earlier one at Stourton and comes to a dead end in Wordsley. Yet another canal was then built to expand the network further: this was the Dudley Canal, which passes through 'Nine Locks' at Brierley Hill. Nine Locks is, in fact, a misnomer - there was such serious congestion at this flight of locks as boats tried to pass through, that in the 1850s the middle seven locks were totally rebuilt and replaced by six locks, making eight locks altogether in the flight. It is still known locally as Nine Locks. Incidentally, a pub at the bottom of the flight is known as the Tenth Lock!

It so happened that the canals were built just in time to carry a particularly fragile commodity for which Stourbridge was to become especially famous - glass. Actually the first glass makers had arrived in the vicinity some years earlier; they were Huguenots fleeing from religious persecution in France in the last years of the 16th century. They began to produce glass for windows and bottles, but it was not until about 200 years later that they started to manufacture the fine tableware for which they have become so famous.

The name of Stuart Crystal, in particular, is associated with Stourbridge glass. By the time Frederick Stuart, who founded the company, was born, there was already an established glass industry in Stourbridge. Frederick was only eleven when he was apprenticed to Richard Bradley Ensell, who owned the Redhouse Glasshouse. Soon afterwards Ensell died, and the business was sold on to the Rufford family; their interests included not just glass-making, but also the production of bricks and banking. This meant that Frederick Stuart acquired a sound all-round commercial training that was to be of great benefit for the future.

In the 1850s he was invited to go into partnership with two other local businessmen, and together they built the Albert Glasshouse in Bridge Street in Wordsley. This was to be the last glasshouse built in the town. Eventually, with four of his sons, Stuart was to establish the company that is so well known today, Stuart & Sons Ltd or Stuart Crystal, as most of us know it, a name that did not actually appear until 1927. This team were to prove to be major innovators in the industry, so much so that in the last years of the 19th century their company alone was producing between 600 and 1,000 new designs a year.

Like so many others, the glass industry has suffered severe setbacks in recent years. Problems really began as long ago as the time between the wars when there was very little market for fine glassware as result of the world-wide depression. During the Second World War the company produced a variety of glass objects, including aircraft landing lights, cathode ray tubes and valves for radar. Even after the war, a number of these specialist products were produced for some years, and this was to enable the company to survive until such times as there was once again a market for high-quality, fine (but expensive) glassware. However, by this time there had been a growth in quality glass-makers around the rest of the world, often in areas with a relatively cheap labour force, so that there was enormous (and fierce) competition for markets.

Sad to say, the excellent quality of its crystal was not enough to enable the company to survive here. Today's Stuart Crystal is produced in Ireland by another well-known name in the crystal industry - Waterford's. Instead, the old industry that made the name of Stourbridge so well known around the world has become a local tourist attraction, based around the Redhouse cone where the young Frederick Stuart began his working career. Here visitors today can learn all about the history of fine glassware, and how it was once produced. It is also possible to watch as people demonstrate how glass was blown and then cut and engraved. At least some of the old skills that gave this town such a special reputation in the past are not being allowed to die out altogether.

However, the future for the town as a market centre is bleak. Where once the town of Stourbridge was considered to be very 'up-market' by comparison with its neighbouring towns in the Black Country, today this relative importance has gone. Many local people would probably say that the decline started in the 1970s, when the town lost its independence and was swallowed up to become part of the Dudley Metropolitan District, moving out from Worcestershire to become part of the 'new' county of the West Midlands.

The movement of people and goods in and around the town had already become difficult from the 1950s; there was constant congestion, especially around the clock tower area at the top of the High Street. Consequently a ring road was eventually built around the heart of the old town in 1969. But this tended to cut off easy access in and out of the main shopping area, and trade there began to decline. Therefore when, in more recent years, the new shopping complex at Merry Hill was built only three miles away (a development which cost some £150 million), it served to put a final nail in the coffin for Stourbridge's shopkeepers. The future for this town as an independent commercial centre is not very bright.

The Centre of Stourbridge

The Town Hall 1931 84683

The Town Hall was built in 1887 at a cost of £5,000 to
commemorate the 50th anniversary of Queen Victoria's accession
to the throne. It sits on the site of a former corn exchange. The
following year, an extension was opened which included a new
corn exchange and council chamber. The signs in front of the
building say 'No Parking' and direct you to the public lavatories.

The Town Hall and Market Street c1960 S213036
Notice the appalling building with the dry cleaning business (left) - fortunately it did not last long, and had already disappeared by the time S213160 was taken. Also, the attractive gas lamps in the earlier picture have all gone. Can you see the small child peeping at the photographer from the doorway on the right?

Market Street c1965 S213160
The building on the left of this picture is the Institute and Social Club, which was opened in 1937. Today the Town Hall, beyond, could be described as a shell fronting the new Crown Centre shopping arcade, which was built in the 1980s. The complex also houses the town's library and various meeting rooms. The earlier sign for public lavatories has now been replaced by a sign which reads, much more bluntly, 'Toilets'.

◄ **St Thomas's Church 1931**
84692
How long does it take to build a church? Work started on the building of St Thomas's in 1728, but it was not actually consecrated until 1866, almost 150 years later; this was because the locals argued with the vicar at Old Swinford, who wanted to install his own man as curate. The building on the left is the church hall, which was built in 1914.

◄ **Market Street c1965** S213159
This photograph is taken further down Market Street. Notice the sign for the car park for the Bell Hotel (left) - the car park sits on what was once advertised as 'the finest and best kept bowling green in the Midlands'. The view has changed little, although the shop beside the road junction, in the centre of the picture in front of the Town Hall, has been replaced.

▼ **The Swimming Baths c1955** S213023
The first swimming baths in Stourbridge opened in 1901. This outdoor pool opened in 1923 and was modernised in 1939. Today the baths are all indoors in the Crystal Leisure Centre which opened in 1989, an appropriate name for a town with a long tradition of producing fine glass. The sign on the railings reads 'Warning - non swimmers not to go beyond this point', although it is difficult to tell which is the shallow and which the deep end.

◄ **The Clock Tower c1955** S213005
This view has really hardly changed in recent years. The building in the centre of the photograph is the Market Hall; today it is really only a façade, as it is now part of the new Crown Centre which adjoins it on the right. The original Market Hall was opened in 1827.

High Street c1960

S213133

The building on the left houses the wine merchants, Nickolls & Perks Ltd, a company that has been in business since 1797 - it is possible to see the date below the window. At the time this photograph was taken, the right-hand side of the building was a pub, the Board Inn, with its door in the centre. In picture number S213167 (page 22-23), this door has been blocked.

◀ **Coventry Street c1965**
S213118
Coventry Street was once known as Pig Street because the pig market was held here; not so long ago, there were many shops here, including five butchers' shops. Behind the buildings on the left stood the first independent chapel to be built in the town, erected in 1698. It was later burnt down in a riot in 1715 and rebuilt, and it survived in use until the end of the 19th century.

High Street from the Mitre Inn c1965 S213167

The words 'Old Bank' inscribed over the entrance of the building in the centre refer to Waldron and Hill, the first bank to open on this site in 1780. The building we see here was erected in 1917. By then the bank had become the London and Midland Bank, and by the 1960s it was a branch of the Midland Bank. The HSBC, as it is now called, has since moved further along the High Street, and today there is a branch of the Yorkshire Bank here.

High Street, the Clock c1965 S213089

This magnificent clock is made of iron and has the words 'This column was constructed at the Stourbridge ironworks 1857' cast into its base. The company had been founded in 1800, and the clock was designed by the works engineer, William Millward. The little sign on the railings in front, however, is an advertisement for a taxi company.

The Mitre Inn c1965 S213170

When this photograph was taken, the government must have just raised the prices of tobacco products or alcohol (probably both!) in a recent budget. One of the signs in the shop window of Alcock's, just across the road, reads 'Beat Rising Prices - No Tax Increase'. I am sure we would wish that even the raised prices were applicable today!

Lower High Street c1960 S213009
In this photograph it is possible to see the detail of the iron work on both the clock itself and the fluted column on which it stands. This is a reminder that there was once an important iron industry here too; the main local products were iron nails and chains.

◀ **High Street and the Gardens c1955** S213008
It is still possible to sit here and watch the world go by today, although this open area once had buildings lining the street between the Market Hall and the Mitre. When one looks at the immaculately maintained gardens here, with flower beds and lawns that require a great deal of attention, it is easy to understand why so many such areas have disappeared from the centre of our towns, sad though it is.

◄ The Mitre Inn c1960
S213057
Today the grass and beds full of flowers have been replaced by paving stones and beds with bushes planted in them instead - all very much easier to maintain. The area serves as the main entrance to the Crown Shopping Centre - this is so-called because there was once a pub here called the Crown.

◄ The Mitre Inn c1950 S213006
A mitre, of course, is the hat worn by a bishop, or sometimes by an abbot. Usually pubs of this name are associated with cathedral towns but this is not always the case, as we can see here. As a collector of pub signs, I am glad to say that the present sign, though changed, is still a very fine depiction of a mitre.

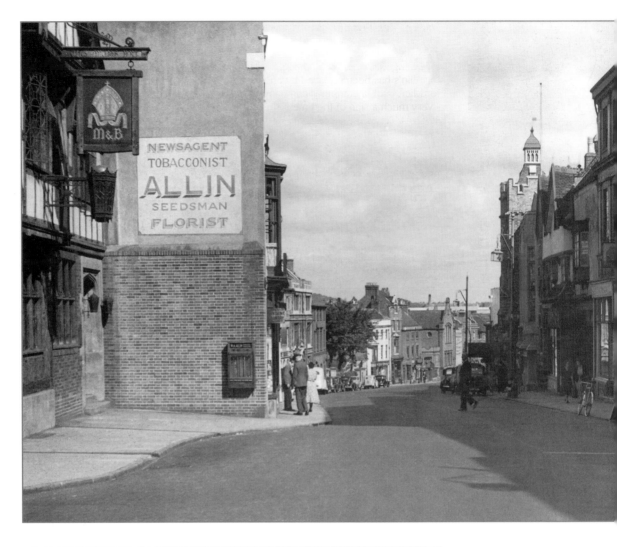

◄ **Lower High Street c1965**
S213162
It is a beautiful sunny summer's day. Yet how interesting that one of the news signboards on the front of Allin's the newsagent's is announcing 'Midland Storm Havoc'. It is no wonder that the British people are said to always talk about the weather.

Lower High Street c1950 S213007

The contraption on the brick wall of Allin's Newsagents beside the pub is a vending machine. Today the sign for Allin's has been replaced by one for Micro Dot, a computer company - very much a sign of the times. This street, which is on the periphery of the main shopping area of Stourbridge, has now become rather run down - a pity, since there are one or two fine houses here dating from the 1700s, built by wealthy local merchants.

▼ The King Edward VI School c1960
S213059

Originally a chantry chapel dating from 1430, the King Edward VI School was founded in 1552, and so is now celebrating its 450th anniversary. The main part of the building, pictured here in the foreground, was built in the 19th century. It is just possible to make out three carved heads under the large window in the centre - in fact there are four heads here altogether, one of which depicts Queen Victoria.

◄ The King Edward VI School c1950
S213004

I particularly admire the extension, a new assembly hall, that was added to the main school building in 1930 (centre). It, too, has some fine carved details - particularly the royal crest in the centre, supported by the English lion and the Welsh dragon. Below it are carved the heads of two kings - Edward VI, in whose reign the school was founded, and George V, who was king when the extension was built.

High Street 1931

84688

Notice the attractive gas lamps along the street; in the later photographs, these have been replaced by tall, unattractive electric lights. The High Street was first macadamised in 1829. It has obviously been recently done again in this picture, because it was used by trams until 1930 and the tram lines have already disappeared. The people in the street need to look where they are walking - there are three ladders leaning against buildings in the picture, two of which have window cleaners on them!

High Street c1950

S213033

The clock is obviously correct - the shadows are very small, and judging by the awnings that are out further down the street, it is a very sunny day. We take clocks on public buildings and shops very much for granted today; Stourbridge only got its first town clock in 1857. This photograph of the High Street and S213010 (page 34) and S213034 (page 35) are taken from the southern end, progressing towards the clock tower at the north.

High Street c1950 S213010

It can sometimes be very difficult with old pictures to work out
exactly where they were each taken - the trick is to look for one or
two 'landmark' buildings. Unfortunately, with this photograph all
the buildings on the left have been replaced, making it very difficult
to work out exactly where we are. The building with the word
'Kings' on it (left) shows the entrance to the King's Hall - the local
cinema at the time.

High Street c1950 S213034

However, in this photograph there are a number of landmarks amongst the buildings on the right, although some have disappeared. Another landmark is the large Lloyds Bank building just beyond the awning on the left. Lloyds Bank was one of many founded in the Midlands in the 18th century, in this case by Sampson Lloyd and John Taylor, who each invested £2,000 in their new company.

High Street 1931
84685
Bordeaux House is a lovely old building. Apart from a balustrade which gives the date of the building (1894), the top floor has now gone. The shop window frames have all recently been painted a gleaming white, which screams at the observer and totally spoils the appearance of the entire building. For years the largest off-licence in the district, today it houses the West Bromwich Building Society.

High Street 1931 84686
The shop on the far left, W Blackburn's, is a butcher's shop; an advertisement in the window reads 'Frigidaire safeguards the food ...', a reminder to us that in the 1930s refrigerators were still very new, and a luxury that few could afford.

High Street c1950 S213012
This photograph was taken at the bottom of the High Street. Notice the people queuing patiently outside the shop on the left. Perhaps they want the fresh bread that is just being delivered from the van parked outside.

High Street c1960 S213054

This is the same section of the High Street as S213012 (previous page), viewed from the other direction. Today the High Street comes to an abrupt end at this point. All the buildings in the middle area of the photograph have gone to make way for the ring road that now surrounds the heart of the town. It is a one-way clockwise ring-road, and it was officially opened on 1 November 1969.

The Public Library c1950 S213011

This is another view that has now changed considerably because of the ring road, which could be said to slash its way through here. E Ward's (left) is just one of many buildings that was demolished when it was built. Today those wanting to cross the road at this point have to use an underpass.

◄ The Public Library and Hagley Road c1955
S213035
Many of the students who trained here were later employed in the glass industry for which the town is so well known. Today the library has moved to the Crown Centre, and this building is part of Stourbridge College, as it is now known.

The Free Library and the War Memorial 1931 84684
The library here should, more correctly, be called the Free Library and Technical Institute. The library was on the ground floor, and was partly funded by a donation of £3,000 given by Andrew Carnegie. The upper floors housed the Institute. It was opened in 1905, and in 1909 the clock tower on the right was added.

The Roman Catholic Church c1965 S213163
The Roman Catholic church of Our Lady and All Saints was designed by E W Pugin and opened in 1864, although the spire (which is 130ft high) was not added until 1889. The church was not actually consecrated, however, until 1891. Today it sits overlooking the new ring road; the road in the foreground, Union Street, has now become a dead end.

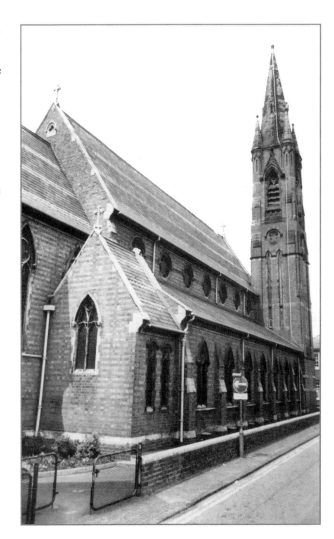

The War Memorial c1965 S213137
This view has gone. The only landmark is the war memorial, and that is now in Mary Stevens Park. There are two particularly fine friezes on the memorial, one showing soldiers walking to the front accompanied by a World War I tank and a despatch rider on his motorbike. The other remembers the Navy, and shows sailors on deck manning a gun.

Kidderminster Road 1931 84689
There is no longer a Kidderminster Road in Stourbridge. From being a relatively quiet road in the 1930s, traffic congestion had already led to it becoming a one-way road in the 1960s with the innovative name of New Road (S213127 page 44). Today this road is a busy three-lane race track, with drivers circling the town and criss-crossing to whichever lane they need.

Kidderminster Road 1931 84689c
This detail shows the workmen from the Stourbridge Gas Department. A gas lamp can be seen just beyond the workmen, with others further down the street. Gas was first introduced in the town in 1833, and the first electricity supply arrived in 1889.

New Road c1965 S213127
To make room for the 'race track', the hedges and trees on the left have all gone. When we compare this picture with 84689 (pages 43-44), it is interesting to see just how much the trees had grown in the thirty years that had passed between. The building on the right is the Methodist church, built in 1928.

Stourbridge's Suburbs

Greenfield Avenue c1955 S213026

Like so many towns, Stourbridge saw tremendous expansion in
the 19th century. This would have been a new development at
that time, and it is still a pleasant road despite its proximity to
the busy main roads close by. It is named Greenfield for a large
house of that name that once stood in the area.

Greenfield Gardens 1931 84698
Sad to say, neither the pond with its fountain nor the bandstand survive here today, and the whole area has been grassed over. If we compare this photograph with S213174 (overleaf), taken some thirty years later, you will see that the trees in the later picture all appear to be younger. New trees were planted when the gardens were redesigned.

▼ **South Road c1965** S213102
Because the ring road around Stourbridge is always so busy, many people
travelling between the west and south-eastern sides of the town prefer to use
South Road. Consequently it too is often very busy. Although there are a number
of older buildings here, this was an area that was to see great expansion during the
period between the wars and in more recent years.

▼ **The Gigmill and the Scout Headquarters c1965** S213105
The building on the right is a pub called the Gigmill. A gigmill was a machine for
raising the nap on cloth, a reminder that woollen cloth production was once an
important industry here. Unfortunately the pub does not have a sign depicting what
a gigmill looked like, which is a pity with such an unusual name.

▲ **Greenfield Gardens
c1965** S213174
Victorian developers were
the first to really
appreciate the need for
green spaces within the
urban sprawl; this was the
first public park in the
town, opened in 1903.
Originally the area was
called Burnt Oak Field,
and then it became
known as Promenade
Gardens, before settling
for its present name.

◄ **Broadway Stores c1965**

S213081

Notice that although this is just a small store for the immediate suburbs, this shop also supplied petrol: there are four pumps on the left supplying different types of Esso petrol - Esso mixture, extra or golden. The shop is still here, and so is the petrol station, although both have grown in size.

Broadway c1965 S213079
This road is typical of 20th-century suburbia almost anywhere in the country. This part of Stourbridge has seen enormous development, particularly in the years after the Second World War. Fortunately, the trees and shrubs in the gardens have grown, softening the landscape considerably, so it no longer looks quite so stark.

Gigmill Way c1965 S213104
Again, this street no longer looks so new. Trees have also been planted in the grass areas bordering the road, giving the entire street a much pleasanter and more welcoming appearance.

South Street Park c1965 S213106
The South Road playing fields were purchased by the town in three separate lots in 1917, 1918 and 1927. Today, with greater awareness of the risk of open water close to playground areas, the water feature on the right has been drained, leaving grassy undulations in the playing field. The distant chimneys, too, have gone.

The Recreation Ground, South Road c1965 S213077
This is a more general view of the South Road Playing Field - the playground can be seen in the distance on the right. On the other side of the tree there is a cement mixer - was this picture taken when the water feature was being demolished, perhaps?

Worcester Street c1965 S213177
This view was taken at the northern end of the Worcester Road; like so many of the others, it was photographed before the ring road was built. The ring road was to go right through the roundabout at the end. We can see the tower of St Thomas's church in Market Street, further into the town.

◄ Mary Stevens Park c1950
S213019
This is a view of Queen's Drive within the park. It was given this name following the visit of the Queen and Prince Philip to Stourbridge in 1957. It is just along here that the war memorial, moved from its position in front of the former library, now stands.

◀ **Mary Stevens Park 1931**

84696

Ernest Stevens, who donated this park to the townspeople of Stourbridge, also donated parkland on the eastern side of the town, known as Stevens Park, for the people of Lye and Wollescote. This one is called Mary Stevens Park as it was expressly dedicated to the memory of his wife. The bandstand shown here still dominates the central area of the park.

▼ **The Entrance Gates to Mary Stevens Park 1931** 84693

These are the main gates to the park, which were modelled on those in front of Buckingham Palace. Notice the lanterns sitting on top of each of the enormous pillars - a sense of their scale can be gained if we notice the man with his bicycle walking through the entrance on the right.

◀ **The Lake, Mary Stevens Park 1931** 84697

Ernest Stevens dedicated the park to be 'a place of rest for the weary, of happiness for children and of beauty for everyone', and this dedication holds true for the bird life too. The lake, which sits on the western side of the park, has become a real haven for birds, particularly since it is not used for boating or other human activities. One hundred years ago, however, it was being used as a swimming pool by the girl's school that was then here.

▼ **Mary Stevens Park, the Children's Playground 1931** 84694
As for today's children, the park is certainly a place of happiness for them. Not only are there the playgrounds, but the paddling pond in the foreground has been drained and replaced by a series of walk-through spurting fountains, which give immeasurable delight to small children on a hot summer's day.

▼ **Mary Stevens Park c1960** S213046
The mansion in the park was originally known as Heath House, and later came to be called Studley Court. For a time it was used as a girl's boarding school; then, during the First World War, it served as a hospital for wounded soldiers. Today these buildings are used as offices, having been converted to house Stourbridge Town Council offices.

▲ **Mary Stevens Park 1931** 84695
The bowling green in the foreground survives, and is still regularly used. However, the surroundings have changed: the hedges and shrubs along the line of the wall in front of the house have grown and thus largely shield it from view.

◀ **Mary Stevens Park c1960**
S213049
The beautiful weather has not only brought the Francis Frith photographer out - the man walking along the path is holding a camera of his own. The large extension with the clock face on it has been added since 84695 was taken.

Norton Road c1955 S213027
This area was once known as the Heath, and it was near here that the only glass works that was really within the town boundaries of Stourbridge was to be found - it closed as early as 1882. Today Norton Road is one of the main roads leading out to the south; because most of the local industry was on the northern side of the town, this became a much smarter part of town in which to live.

Racecourse Lane, Pedmore c1965 S213152
Despite the name, there is no longer a racecourse here. This road could be said to define the southern boundary of the town. Notice the newly laid strip of tarmac along the middle of the road where the road has recently been dug up - some things never seem to change!

The Golf Club c1965 S213139
Stourbridge's Golf Club lies adjacent to Racecourse Lane, with the club house at the eastern end, looking today almost exactly as it did when this photograph was taken. The club was founded in 1892, and by 1909 it had expanded so that it had an 18-hole course.

Worcester Lane, Pedmore c1965 S213153
The spire in the distance has now gone. It was on top of St Mary's church in Old Swinford. Otherwise this street has hardly changed at all in the intervening years, except that the trees are even more well established now than then.

◀ **Hagley Road c1950**
S213031
Once one of several turnpike roads around the town, today Hagley Road is the main road leading out of Stourbridge to the south; it also links up with a number of other major road systems surrounding the Birmingham conurbation. This means that it is always extremely busy, a far cry from the peaceful scene shown here.

◀ **Hagley Road c1950**
S213032
The sign on the building across the road is for Stour Valley Motors, where Austin and Ford cars are sold or serviced. Today this photograph appears remarkable because there is not one line painted anywhere on the road - we have become so used to markings that tell us where we can and cannot drive or park!

◀ **Glasshouse Hill c1950**
S213029
Once known as the Malt Shovel, the pub sitting by the road junction is now called the Labour in Vain. Originally a pub of this name meant that the quality of the beer available at the pub was so high that rival landlords would 'labour in vain' to produce a brew that was as good.

Town and Country Beyond Stourbridge

Old Swinford, The Labour in Vain c1955
051013
Look more closely at the pub sign, however. Today such signs are usually thought to be totally politically incorrect; but in fact, the joke is on the ladies, who in their ignorance can be seen in the picture labouring in vain to wash a black man white! There is no picture sign here today, unfortunately.

◀ **Old Swinford, The Hospital c1965** 051005 Although called a hospital, this is in fact a school; it was founded in the 17th century by a local benefactor called Thomas Foley, who had made his fortune as an iron master. The large sign, incidentally, quotes the 1932 Rights of Way Act, and warns trespassers that this is a private driveway and not a public right of way.

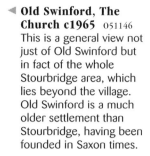

◄ **Old Swinford, The Church c1965** 051146
This is a general view not just of Old Swinford but in fact of the whole Stourbridge area, which lies beyond the village. Old Swinford is a much older settlement than Stourbridge, having been founded in Saxon times.

▼ **Old Swinford, Hagley Road c1955** 051015
I particularly like the advertisement here for Goodwin's 'Extra' Flour with the words 'Good Quality Wins' written at the bottom (left). The baby lying on its back and kicking its feet in the air would appear to me to suggest that the flour could have a secondary use as talcum powder! I am sure that was not what was meant, though.

◄ **Old Swinford, Hagley Road c1955** 051014
The buildings on the right between the telegraph poles have all been removed to make way for a large Tesco petrol station and convenience store, a new style of shop from this particular supermarket company that are now beginning to appear all over the country.

Old Swinford, The Church 1931 84691

St Mary's church was the earliest church in the area, serving Old Swinford long before there was any settlement in Stourbridge. The church dates from at least the 13th century, although it has been constantly restored and altered over the centuries. The spire on top has now gone, however, having been recently dismantled because it had become unsafe.

West Hagley, Hagley Hall c1960 W305041
Hagley Hall is a beautiful Palladian style mansion that was designed by Sanderson Miller and built in the mid 18th century. It suffered a terrible fire in 1925 which destroyed part of the house and many of its contents. Fortunately it has since been restored, and is now open to the public. This view shows the rear of the house.

West Hagley, The Lyttelton Arms c1965 W305043
The pub here is named for the Lyttelton family, owners of nearby Hagley Hall. It was the 1st Lord Lyttelton who was responsible for the house and grounds we see today. He was at one time the Chancellor of the Exchequer. The 2nd Lord, nicknamed Naughty Tom, was one of the founders of the notorious Hell Fire Club.

**West Hagley
Worcester Road
c1955** W305026
This view has changed little in recent years. The house with the ivy on its wall is now the home of Hagley Homeopathy. Notice the numerous advertisements for different tobacco products - Wills' Gold Flake, Wills' Cut Golden Bar, Players and one for Craven A over the shop door.

◄ **West Hagley, The Cross Keys c1950** W305006
The Cross Keys pub stands behind the parked vehicles. Today the pub has been converted into cottages, but the name survives, because they are called Cross Keys Mews. The garage survives too, overlooking the very busy intersection where roads diverge to go to Kidderminster or Worcester.

◄ **West Hagley, Worcester Road c1960** W305032
The store that was Bridge's shop in W305026 (pages 68-69) is now five years later run by F Park. Today it is a Victoria Wine shop. The private houses next door are now also all occupied by shops. The gateway on the right is an entrance to playing fields, which can still be found behind the buildings.

▼ **Clent, Early Morning over the Clent Hills c1955** C330007
Along with the nearby Lickey Hills, the Clent Hills (which rise to 1,000 ft above sea level) form a clear boundary between rural countryside to the south and west and the man-made industrial landscape to the north-east. There is a toposcope just beside the Four Stones which was erected in 1929 by the Rotary Clubs of Stourbridge and Kidderminster.

◄ **Blakedown, Birmingham Road 1968** B419011
The shop window has a display of boats and a poster asking 'When will Alec Rose arrive?' The photograph must therefore date from the summer of 1968, when Alec Rose, a 59-year-old greengrocer from Portsmouth, completed his single-handed voyage around the world in his yacht the 'Lively Lady'. Another poster advertises a June garden fete.

Cookley, Lea Castle Gates c1950 C333022
These rather pretty buildings are known as the North Lodges, and sit beside the Wolverhampton Road. It would appear that this entrance was seldom used when this photograph was taken; today, however, there is a tarmac road leading through the gateway.

Cookley, The Square c1950 C333017
Originally called the Spin Eagle, the pub at the far end of the street was renamed the Eagle and Spur in 1870. Today it is known as the Eagle in Cookley, and has moved next door following the demolition of the building it occupies here. This photograph serves to remind us of how much more peaceful life was then in such villages - today no dog standing in the middle of the road would survive for very long!

Caunsall, The Rock Tavern c1950 C761008
One would hardly call this a tavern today; it is now very much more of a country inn sitting overlooking a road that seems much narrower now, with hardly room for two-way traffic to squeeze past when vehicles meet.

Caunsall, The Anchor c1950 C761015
As a collector of pub signs, the first thing I notice here is the wonderful anchor sign, today replaced by a standard picture sign. It seems strange to have a pub of this name right in the middle of England, but in fact Caunsall overlooks the River Stour. The river has long been used for boats trading upstream and, more importantly, downstream, where the Stour links up with the River Severn and thus with the ports of Gloucester and Bristol.

Kinver, A Cave Dwelling 1931 84708
The hills around Kinver are made of soft, easily cut sandstone, and they have provided cave dwellings for centuries. Most such homes were abandoned in the late 19th century, but this one would appear to have been still occupied, with curtains in the window. One cave house even had a chimney flue cut all the way up through the rock above it.

Kinver, High Street 1931 84702
Because of the attraction of the caves and the walks along Kinver Edge, the town became such a popular local resort that in 1901 a small railway line was opened linking the village with Stourbridge, Birmingham and all the Black Country. On Whit Monday Bank Holiday in 1905 the railway had its highest ever number of passengers - 16,699 people in all. Sad to say, the line closed in 1930.

▼ Kinver, Hyde Lock c1955 K37303

Although of course built for the transportation of goods, the canal here is still very busy; but now it is holidaymakers who use it. The canal is the Staffordshire and Worcestershire Canal, linking the River Severn with the Potteries. The title of 'Hyde Lock' for the photograph is correct - the lock is just on the other side of the bridge.

▼ Potter's Cross, The Village c1965 P352001

Kinver and Potter's Cross, both once individual small villages, have now grown so that today Potter's Cross could really be said to be a part of Kinver. This is the junction for roads coming from the north travelling towards Kinver itself.

▲ Kinver, Ye Olde White Harte Hotel c1955

K37024

Originally an old coaching inn, the White Hart is thought to date from the early 1600s. It looks much the worse for wear in this later photograph. However, in more recent years it has had a face lift, and is now looking much smarter and more welcoming than it does in this photograph or in 84702 (previous page).

◀ **Potter's Cross, The Village c1965** P352004
Although the painted sign on the wall has almost completely faded away, it is still possible to buy food at the Café - it is now a Chinese takeaway!

Wollaston, The Centre c1960 W239006
There's an election taking place - one of the three posters on the right is asking the local people to 'Vote for Frank Spiller'. I love the name of the tea being sold in D Hadlington's corner shop - Mazawattee tea sounds really exotic. The shop also sells Bournville cocoa, which, of course, will have been produced in Bournville, only a few miles from here.

Wollaston, St James's Church c1960 W239001
St James's church was built in 1860; it is rather unusual, having been made from black (or some would say 'blue') bricks. These contrast very effectively with the light stonework detailing around the windows and on the tower, so that the whole effect is quite stunning.

Amblecote, Holy Trinity Church c1965 S213114
It was in Amblecote that the local glass industry was centred. Today it is separated from the heart of Stourbridge only by the modern ring road. Holy Trinity church is another of the many churches in the area that were built in Victorian times, a period that saw an enormous growth in the local population and hence a demand for many new churches. This church dates from the 1840s, and was designed by Samuel Heming.

Kingswinford, The Shopping Precinct c1965
K84009
This shopping precinct overlooks the Cross, a pub name that has also been given to the main road junction in the centre of the town. The electricity showroom on the right, where 'Better things are electric' (according to a sign in the window), is an extremely futuristic-looking building; it still has not, to my mind, settled into its place.

◄ Wordsley, High Street c1965
W240055

Notice the petrol pump just beside the shop: it sits by the entrance to a garage, and today would be considered a very dangerous fire hazard in such a position. Difficult though it is to imagine now, the name Wordsley originally meant that this settlement was once a woodland clearing belonging to a man named Wulfweard.

▼ Kingswinford, The Parish Church of St Mary c1965 K84012

St Mary's church dates from the 12th century, when it served a parish of over 7,000 acres, including present-day Brierley Hill. It sits some distance away from the Cross: although the original village would have been here, commercial needs meant that the village migrated towards the road that linked Wolverhampton with Stourbridge, where, presumably, there was better potential for trade.

◄ Kingswinford, The Old Court House Hotel c1965 K84014

This pub, just across the road from the church, was once the town's courthouse. When sentences were passed here, they would then, it is said, be announced publicly from an old medieval preaching cross which once stood in the churchyard.

Brierley Hill, High Street 1968 B355018 Brierley Hill was a relatively late town. It is first described as being an inhabited settlement only in 1619, when squatters began to move on to what was then common land. Within 200 years it had become a major industrial centre, with forges, brick-kilns, glass-works and nail workshops.

Brierley Hill, Delph Locks c1965 B355004
The word 'delph' refers to shallow workings of open coal pits, which are dotted all around this locality. The locks here were built by the Dudley Canal Company to link their canal system with the Stourbridge Canal. Although originally built in 1779, the system of locks here was completely rebuilt in 1858, when the number of locks was dropped from nine to eight.

Lye, High Street c1965 L178004
Frequently known as 'the Lye', this small town has been described as 'the last place God ever made', apparently because so much of it was once waste ground! The first people to live here built their houses from mud (the area later became an important centre for brick production), so that Lye came to be known as the 'Mud City'.

Index

Frith Book Co Titles

www.francisfrith.co.uk

The Frith Book Company publishes over 100 new titles each year. A selection of those currently available are listed below. For latest catalogue please contact Frith Book Co.

Town Books 96 pages, approx 100 photos. County and Themed Books 128 pages, approx 150 photos (unless specified). All titles hardback laminated case and jacket except those indicated pb (paperback)

Amersham, Chesham & Rickmansworth (pb)			Derby (pb)	1-85937-367-4	£9.99
	1-85937-340-2	£9.99	Derbyshire (pb)	1-85937-196-5	£9.99
Ancient Monuments & Stone Circles	1-85937-143-4	£17.99	Devon (pb)	1-85937-297-x	£9.99
Aylesbury (pb)	1-85937-227-9	£9.99	Dorset (pb)	1-85937-269-4	£9.99
Bakewell	1-85937-113-2	£12.99	Dorset Churches	1-85937-172-8	£17.99
Barnstaple (pb)	1-85937-300-3	£9.99	Dorset Coast (pb)	1-85937-299-6	£9.99
Bath (pb)	1-85937419-0	£9.99	Dorset Living Memories	1-85937-210-4	£14.99
Bedford (pb)	1-85937-205-8	£9.99	Down the Severn	1-85937-118-3	£14.99
Berkshire (pb)	1-85937-191-4	£9.99	Down the Thames (pb)	1-85937-278-3	£9.99
Berkshire Churches	1-85937-170-1	£17.99	Down the Trent	1-85937-311-9	£14.99
Blackpool (pb)	1-85937-382-8	£9.99	Dublin (pb)	1-85937-231-7	£9.99
Bognor Regis (pb)	1-85937-431-x	£9.99	East Anglia (pb) ✓	1-85937-265-1	£9.99
Bournemouth	1-85937-067-5	£12.99	East London	1-85937-080-2	£14.99
Bradford (pb)	1-85937-204-x	£9.99	East Sussex	1-85937-130-2	£14.99
Brighton & Hove(pb)	1-85937-192-2	£8.99	Eastbourne	1-85937-061-6	£12.99
Bristol (pb)	1-85937-264-3	£9.99	Edinburgh (pb)	1-85937-193-0	£8.99
British Life A Century Ago (pb)	1-85937-213-9	£9.99	England in the 1880s	1-85937-331-3	£17.99
Buckinghamshire (pb)	1-85937-200-7	£9.99	English Castles (pb)	1-85937-434-4	£9.99
Camberley (pb)	1-85937-222-8	£9.99	English Country Houses	1-85937-161-2	£17.99
Cambridge (pb)	1-85937-422-0	£9.99	Essex (pb)	1-85937-270-8	£9.99
Cambridgeshire (pb)	1-85937-420-4	£9.99	Exeter	1-85937-126-4	£12.99
Canals & Waterways (pb)	1-85937-291-0	£9.99	Exmoor	1-85937-132-9	£14.99
Canterbury Cathedral (pb)	1-85937-179-5	£9.99	Falmouth	1-85937-066-7	£12.99
Cardiff (pb)	1-85937-093-4	£9.99	Folkestone (pb)	1-85937-124-8	£9.99
Carmarthenshire	1-85937-216-3	£14.99	Glasgow (pb)	1-85937-190-6	£9.99
Chelmsford (pb)	1-85937-310-0	£9.99	Gloucestershire	1-85937-102-7	£14.99
Cheltenham (pb)	1-85937-095-0	£9.99	Great Yarmouth (pb)	1-85937-426-3	£9.99
Cheshire (pb)	1-85937-271-6	£9.99	Greater Manchester (pb)	1-85937-266-x	£9.99
Chester	1-85937-090-x	£12.99	Guildford (pb)	1-85937-410-7	£9.99
Chesterfield	1-85937-378-x	£9.99	Hampshire (pb)	1-85937-279-1	£9.99
Chichester (pb)	1-85937-228-7	£9.99	Hampshire Churches (pb)	1-85937-207-4	£9.99
Colchester (pb)	1-85937-188-4	£8.99	Harrogate	1-85937-423-9	£9.99
Cornish Coast	1-85937-163-9	£14.99	Hastings & Bexhill (pb)	1-85937-131-0	£9.99
Cornwall (pb)	1-85937-229-5	£9.99	Heart of Lancashire (pb)	1-85937-197-3	£9.99
Cornwall Living Memories	1-85937-248-1	£14.99	Helston (pb)	1-85937-214-7	£9.99
Cotswolds (pb)	1-85937-230-9	£9.99	Hereford (pb)	1-85937-175-2	£9.99
Cotswolds Living Memories	1-85937-255-4	£14.99	Herefordshire	1-85937-174-4	£14.99
County Durham	1-85937-123-x	£14.99	Hertfordshire (pb)	1-85937-247-3	£9.99
Croydon Living Memories	1-85937-162-0	£9.99	Horsham (pb)	1-85937-432-8	£9.99
Cumbria	1-85937-101-9	£14.99	Humberside	1-85937-215-5	£14.99
Dartmoor	1-85937-145-0	£14.99	Hythe, Romney Marsh & Ashford	1-85937-256-2	£9.99

Available from your local bookshop or from the publisher

Frith Book Co Titles (continued)

Title	ISBN	Price	Title	ISBN	Price
Ipswich (pb)	1-85937-424-7	£9.99	St Ives (pb)	1-85937415-8	£9.99
Ireland (pb)	1-85937-181-7	£9.99	Scotland (pb)	1-85937-182-5	£9.99
Isle of Man (pb)	1-85937-268-6	£9.99	Scottish Castles (pb)	1-85937-323-2	£9.99
Isles of Scilly	1-85937-136-1	£14.99	Sevenoaks & Tunbridge	1-85937-057-8	£12.99
Isle of Wight (pb)	1-85937-429-8	£9.99	Sheffield, South Yorks (pb)	1-85937-267-8	£9.99
Isle of Wight Living Memories	1-85937-304-6	£14.99	Shrewsbury (pb)	1-85937-325-9	£9.99
Kent (pb)	1-85937-189-2	£9.99	Shropshire (pb)	1-85937-326-7	£9.99
Kent Living Memories	1-85937-125-6	£14.99	Somerset	1-85937-153-1	£14.99
Lake District (pb)	1-85937-275-9	£9.99	South Devon Coast	1-85937-107-8	£14.99
Lancaster, Morecambe & Heysham (pb)	1-85937-233-3	£9.99	South Devon Living Memories	1-85937-168-x	£14.99
Leeds (pb)	1-85937-202-3	£9.99	South Hams	1-85937-220-1	£14.99
Leicester	1-85937-073-x	£12.99	Southampton (pb)	1-85937-427-1	£9.99
Leicestershire (pb)	1-85937-185-x	£9.99	Southport (pb)	1-85937-425-5	£9.99
Lincolnshire (pb)	1-85937-433-6	£9.99	Staffordshire	1-85937-047-0	£12.99
Liverpool & Merseyside (pb)	1-85937-234-1	£9.99	Stratford upon Avon	1-85937-098-5	£12.99
London (pb)	1-85937-183-3	£9.99	Suffolk (pb)	1-85937-221-x	£9.99
Ludlow (pb)	1-85937-176-0	£9.99	Suffolk Coast	1-85937-259-7	£14.99
Luton (pb)	1-85937-235-x	£9.99	Surrey (pb)	1-85937-240-6	£9.99
Maidstone	1-85937-056-x	£14.99	Sussex (pb)	1-85937-184-1	£9.99
Manchester (pb)	1-85937-198-1	£9.99	Swansea (pb)	1-85937-167-1	£9.99
Middlesex	1-85937-158-2	£14.99	Tees Valley & Cleveland	1-85937-211-2	£14.99
New Forest	1-85937-128-0	£14.99	Thanet (pb)	1-85937-116-7	£9.99
Newark (pb)	1-85937-366-6	£9.99	Tiverton (pb)	1-85937-178-7	£9.99
Newport, Wales (pb)	1-85937-258-9	£9.99	Torbay	1-85937-063-2	£12.99
Newquay (pb)	1-85937-421-2	£9.99	Truro	1-85937-147-7	£12.99
Norfolk (pb)	1-85937-195-7	£9.99	Victorian and Edwardian Cornwall	1-85937-252-x	£14.99
Norfolk Living Memories	1-85937-217-1	£14.99	Victorian & Edwardian Devon	1-85937-253-8	£14.99
Northamptonshire	1-85937-150-7	£14.99	Victorian & Edwardian Kent	1-85937-149-3	£14.99
Northumberland Tyne & Wear (pb)	1-85937-281-3	£9.99	Vic & Ed Maritime Album	1-85937-144-2	£17.99
North Devon Coast	1-85937-146-9	£14.99	Victorian and Edwardian Sussex	1-85937-157-4	£14.99
North Devon Living Memories	1-85937-261-9	£14.99	Victorian & Edwardian Yorkshire	1-85937-154-x	£14.99
North London	1-85937-206-6	£14.99	Victorian Seaside	1-85937-159-0	£17.99
North Wales (pb)	1-85937-298-8	£9.99	Villages of Devon (pb)	1-85937-293-7	£9.99
North Yorkshire (pb)	1-85937-236-8	£9.99	Villages of Kent (pb)	1-85937-294-5	£9.99
Norwich (pb)	1-85937-194-9	£8.99	Villages of Sussex (pb)	1-85937-295-3	£9.99
Nottingham (pb)	1-85937-324-0	£9.99	Warwickshire (pb)	1-85937-203-1	£9.99
Nottinghamshire (pb)	1-85937-187-6	£9.99	Welsh Castles (pb)	1-85937-322-4	£9.99
Oxford (pb)	1-85937-411-5	£9.99	West Midlands (pb)	1-85937-289-9	£9.99
Oxfordshire (pb)	1-85937-430-1	£9.99	West Sussex	1-85937-148-5	£14.99
Peak District (pb)	1-85937-280-5	£9.99	West Yorkshire (pb)	1-85937-201-5	£9.99
Penzance	1-85937-069-1	£12.99	Weymouth (pb)	1-85937-209-0	£9.99
Peterborough (pb)	1-85937-219-8	£9.99	Wiltshire (pb)	1-85937-277-5	£9.99
Piers	1-85937-237-6	£17.99	Wiltshire Churches (pb)	1-85937-171-x	£9.99
Plymouth	1-85937-119-1	£12.99	Wiltshire Living Memories	1-85937-245-7	£14.99
Poole & Sandbanks (pb)	1-85937-251-1	£9.99	Winchester (pb)	1-85937-428-x	£9.99
Preston (pb)	1-85937-212-0	£9.99	Windmills & Watermills	1-85937-242-2	£17.99
Reading (pb)	1-85937-238-4	£9.99	Worcester (pb)	1-85937-165-5	£9.99
Romford (pb)	1-85937-319-4	£9.99	Worcestershire	1-85937-152-3	£14.99
Salisbury (pb)	1-85937-239-2	£9.99	York (pb)	1-85937-199-x	£9.99
Scarborough (pb)	1-85937-379-8	£9.99	Yorkshire (pb)	1-85937-186-8	£9.99
St Albans (pb)	1-85937-341-0	£9.99	Yorkshire Living Memories	1-85937-166-3	£14.99

See Frith books on the internet www.francisfrith.co.uk

FRITH PRODUCTS & SERVICES

Francis Frith would doubtless be pleased to know that the pioneering publishing venture he started in 1860 still continues today. A hundred and forty years later, The Francis Frith Collection continues in the same innovative tradition and is now one of the foremost publishers of vintage photographs in the world. Some of the current activities include:

Interior Decoration

Today Frith's photographs can be seen framed and as giant wall murals in thousands of pubs, restaurants, hotels, banks, retail stores and other public buildings throughout the country. In every case they enhance the unique local atmosphere of the places they depict and provide reminders of gentler days in an increasingly busy and frenetic world.

Product Promotions

Frith products are used by many major companies to promote the sales of their own products or to reinforce their own history and heritage. Frith promotions have been used by Hovis bread, Courage beers, Scots Porage Oats, Colman's mustard, Cadbury's foods, Mellow Birds coffee, Dunhill pipe tobacco, Guinness, and Bulmer's Cider.

Genealogy and Family History

As the interest in family history and roots grows world-wide, more and more people are turning to Frith's photographs of Great Britain for images of the towns, villages and streets where their ancestors lived; and, of course, photographs of the churches and chapels where their ancestors were christened, married and buried are an essential part of every genealogy tree and family album.

Frith Products

All Frith photographs are available Framed or just as Mounted Prints and Posters (size 23 x 16 inches). These may be ordered from the address below. From time to time other products - Address Books, Calendars, Table Mats, etc - are available.

The Internet

Already twenty thousand Frith photographs can be viewed and purchased on the internet through the Frith websites and a myriad of partner sites.

For more detailed information on Frith companies and products, look at these sites:

www.francisfrith.co.uk
www.francisfrith.com
(for North American visitors)

See the complete list of Frith Books at:

www.francisfrith.co.uk

This web site is regularly updated with the latest list of publications from the Frith Book Company. If you wish to buy books relating to another part of the country that your local bookshop does not stock, you may purchase on-line.

For further information, trade, or author enquiries please contact us at the address below:
The Francis Frith Collection, Frith's Barn, Teffont, Salisbury, Wiltshire, England SP3 5QP.
Tel: +44 (0)1722 716 376 Fax: +44 (0)1722 716 881 Email: sales@francisfrith.co.uk

See Frith books on the internet www.francisfrith.co.uk

TO RECEIVE YOUR FREE MOUNTED PRINT

Mounted Print
Overall size 14 x 11 inches

Cut out this Voucher and return it with your remittance for £2.25 to cover postage and handling, to UK addresses. For overseas addresses please include £4.00 post and handling. Choose any photograph included in this book. Your SEPIA print will be A4 in size, and mounted in a cream mount with burgundy rule line, overall size 14 x 11 inches.

Order additional Mounted Prints at HALF PRICE (only £7.49 each*)

If there are further pictures you would like to order, possibly as gifts for friends and family, purchase them at half price (no additional postage and handling required).

Have your Mounted Prints framed*

For an additional £14.95 per print you can have your chosen Mounted Print framed in an elegant polished wood and gilt moulding, overall size 16 x 13 inches (no additional postage and handling required).

---

* IMPORTANT!
These special prices are only available if ordered using the original voucher on this page (no copies permitted) and at the same time as your free Mounted Print, for delivery to the same address

---

Frith Collectors' Guild

From time to time we publish a magazine of news and stories about Frith photographs and further special offers of Frith products. If you would like 12 months FREE membership, please return this form.

Send completed forms to:
**The Francis Frith Collection,
Frith's Barn, Teffont, Salisbury,
Wiltshire SP3 5QP**

Voucher for FREE and Reduced Price Frith Prints

Picture no.	Page number	Qty	Mounted @ £7.49	Framed + £14.95	Total Cost
		1	Free of charge*	£	£
			£7.49	£	£
			£7.49	£	£
			£7.49	£	£
			£7.49	£	£
			£7.49	£	£

Please allow 28 days for delivery   *** Post & handling**   £2.25

Book Title . . . .   **Total Order Cost**   £

Please do not photocopy this voucher. Only the original is valid, so please cut it out and return it to us.

I enclose a cheque / postal order for £ . . . .
made payable to 'The Francis Frith Collection'
OR please debit my Mastercard / Visa / Switch / Amex card
(credit cards please on all overseas orders)

Number . . . .

Issue No(Switch only) . . . . .Valid from (Amex/Switch) . . . .

Expires . . . .   Signature . . . .

Name Mr/Mrs/Ms . . . .

Address . . . .

. . . .

. . . .

Postcode . . . . Daytime Tel No . . . .

Email Address . . . .

Valid to 31/12/04

The Francis Frith Collectors' Guild

Please enrol me as a member for 12 months free of charge.

Name Mr/Mrs/Ms . . . .

Address . . . .

. . . .

. . . . Postcode . . . .

Would you like to find out more about Francis Frith?

We have recently recruited some entertaining speakers who are happy to visit local groups, clubs and societies to give an illustrated talk documenting Frith's travels and photographs. If you are a member of such a group and are interested in hosting a presentation, we would love to hear from you.

Our speakers bring with them a small selection of our local town and county books, together with sample prints. They are happy to take orders. A small proportion of the order value is donated to the group who have hosted the presentation. The talks are therefore an excellent way of fundraising for small groups and societies.

Can you help us with information about any of the Frith photographs in this book?

We are gradually compiling an historical record for each of the photographs in the Frith archive. It is always fascinating to find out the names of the people shown in the pictures, as well as insights into the shops, buildings and other features depicted.

If you recognize anyone in the photographs in this book, or if you have information not already included in the author's caption, do let us know. We would love to hear from you, and will try to publish it in future books or articles.

Our production team

Frith books are produced by a small dedicated team at offices in the converted Grade II listed 18th-century barn at Teffont near Salisbury, illustrated above. Most have worked with the Frith Collection for many years. All have in common one quality: they have a passion for the Frith Collection. The team is constantly expanding, but currently includes:

Jason Buck, John Buck, Douglas Burns, Ruth Butler, Heather Crisp, Isobel Hall, Hazel Heaton, Peter Horne, James Kinnear, Tina Leary, Hannah Marsh, Sue Molloy, Kate Rotondetto, Dean Scource, Eliza Sackett, Terence Sackett, Sandra Sanger, Lewis Taylor, Shelley Tolcher, Clive Wathen and Jenny Wathen.